By Rebecca Hankin

Prepared under the direction of Robert Hillerich, Ph.D.

Library of Congress Cataloging in Publication Data

Hankin, Rebecca.
I can be a doctor.

Summary: Describes in simple terms the training and duties of a doctor.
1. Medicine—Vocational guidance—Juvenile literature.
2. Physicians—Juvenile Literature. [1. Physicians.
2. Occupations.] I. Title.
R690.H364 1985 610.69'52 84-23304
ISBN 0-516-01846-9

Printed in the United States of America.
1 2 3 4 5 6 7 8 9 10 R 94 93 92 91 90 89 88 87 86 85

PICTURE DICTIONARY

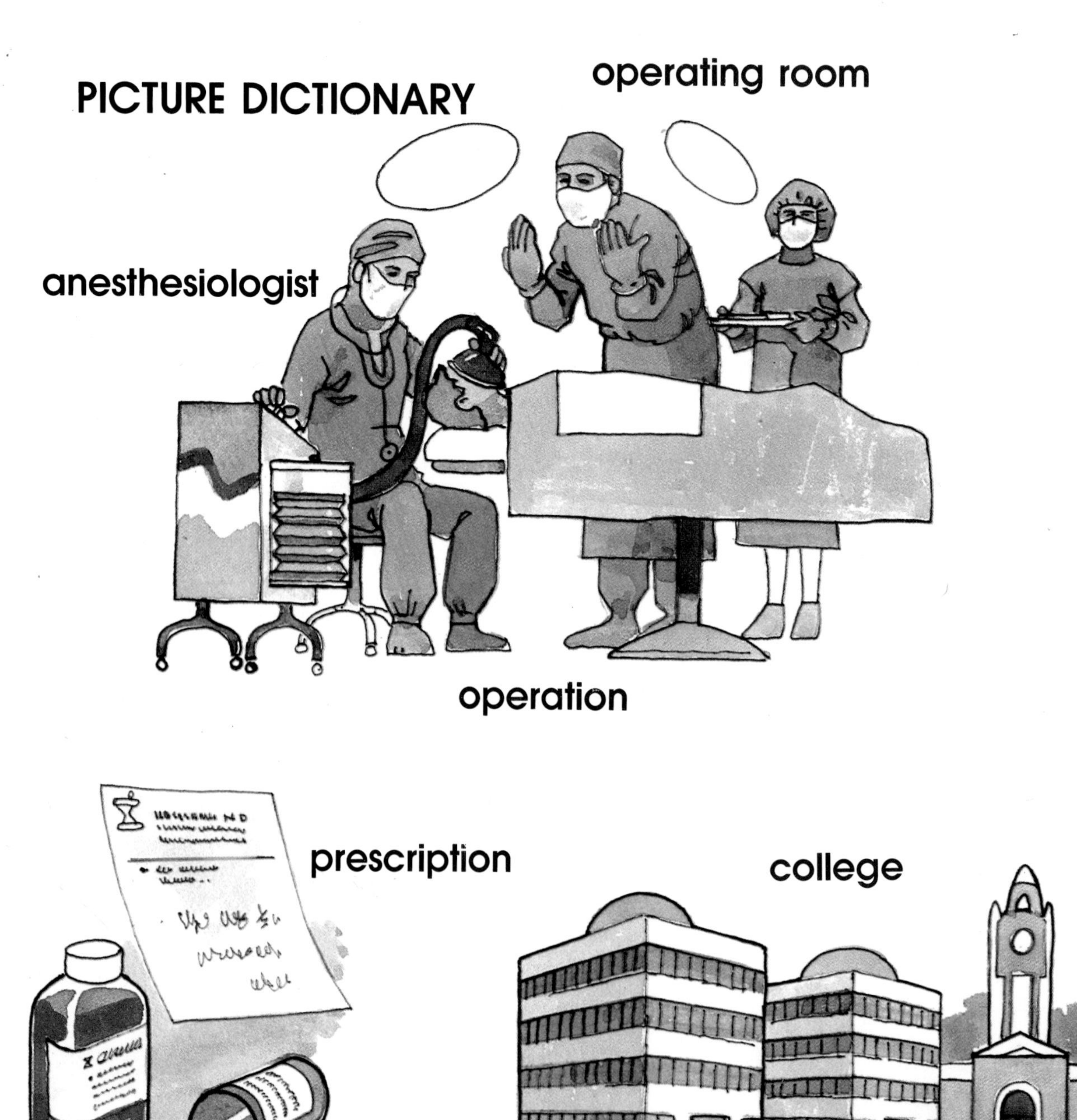

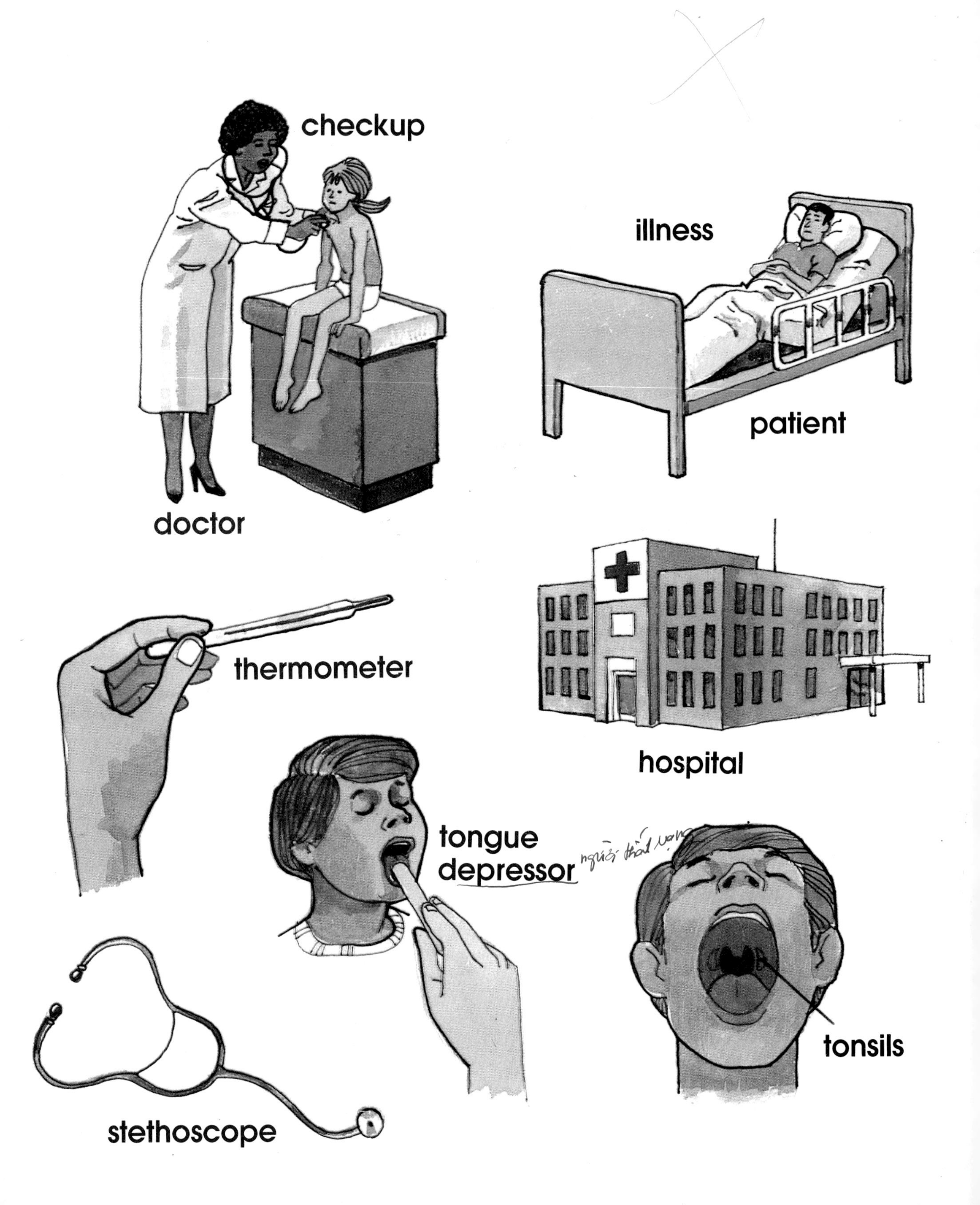
checkup
illness
patient
doctor
thermometer
hospital
tongue
depressor
tonsils
stethoscope

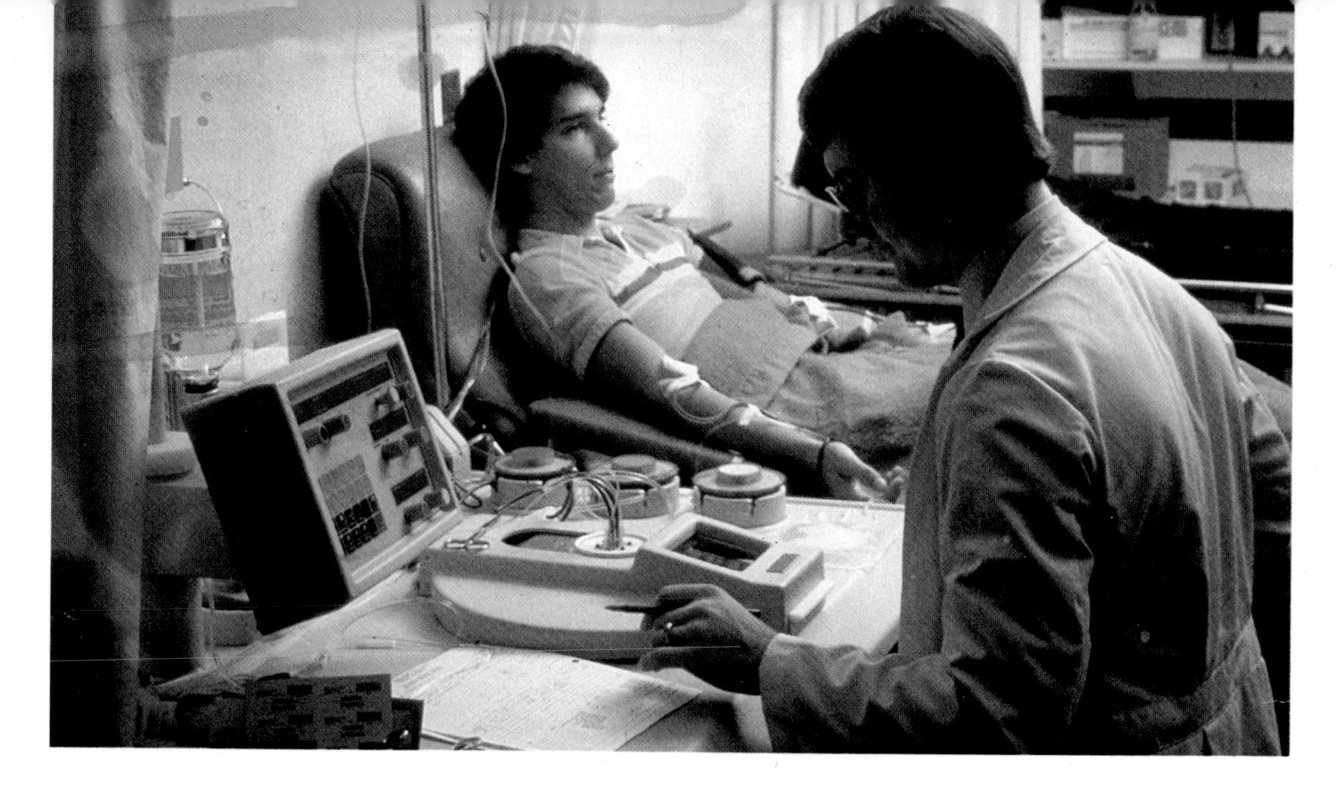

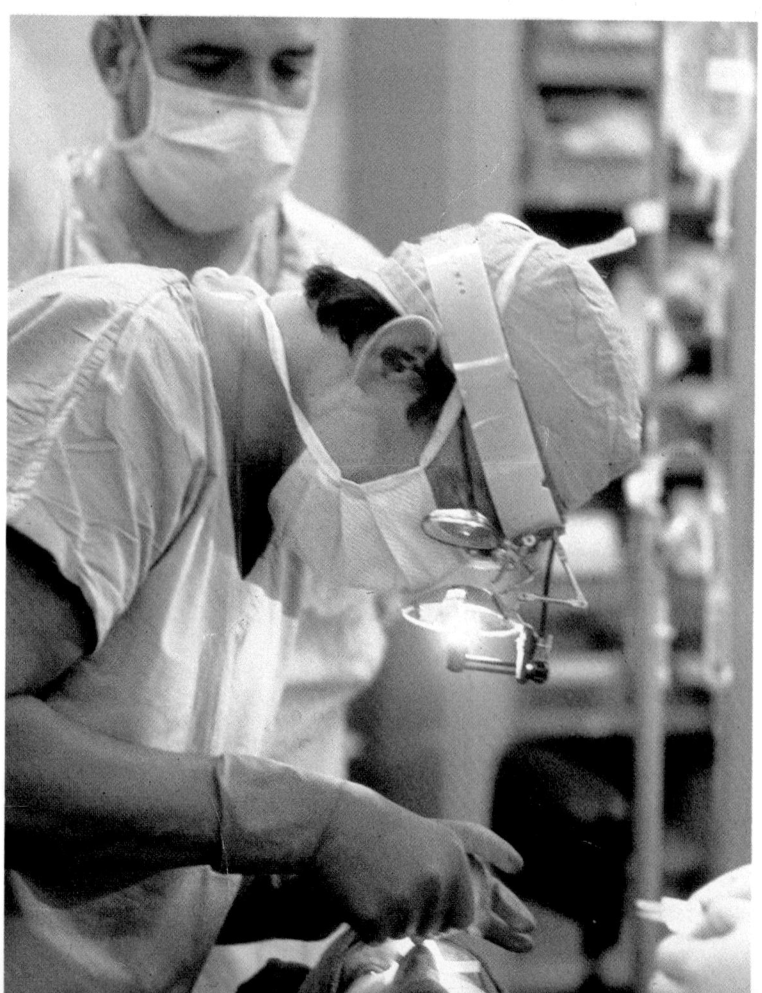

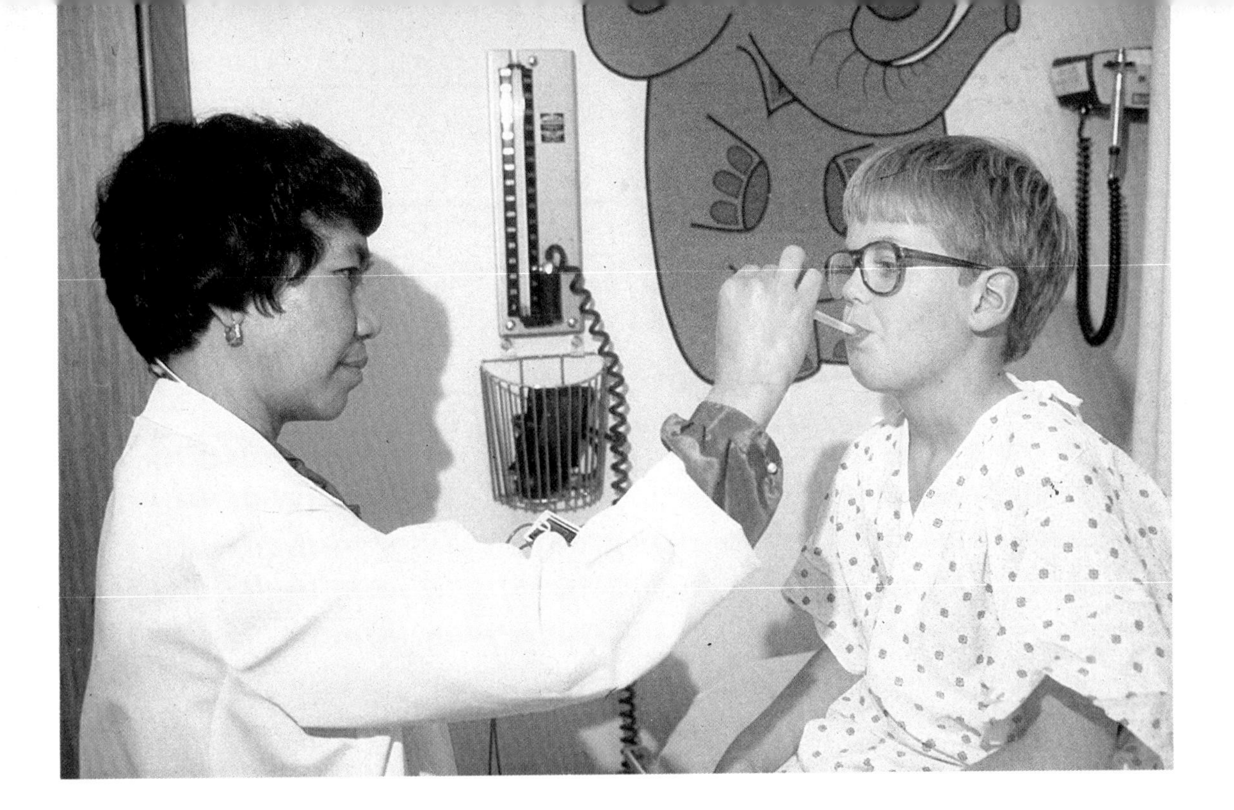

Doctors are special people. They help us to be healthy.

Sometimes you get sick. You might have a headache or feel hot. Maybe you have a bad cold.

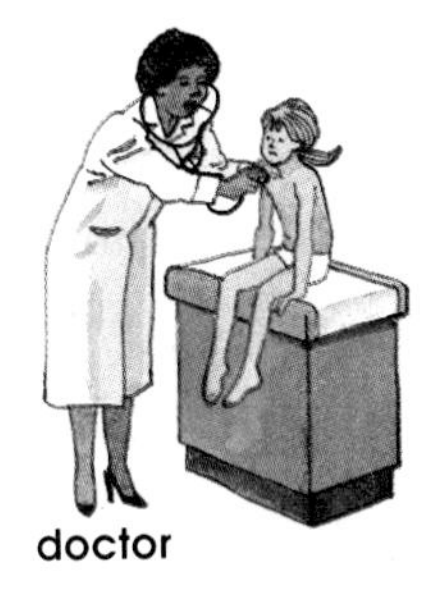
doctor

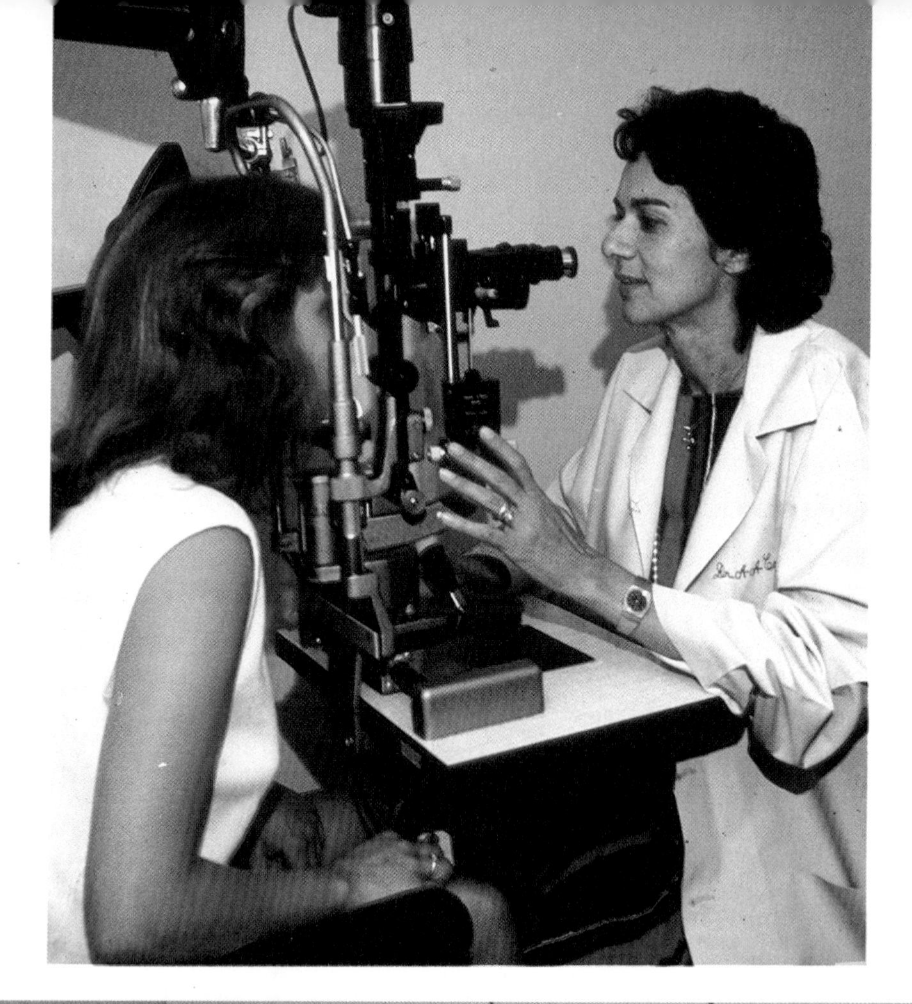

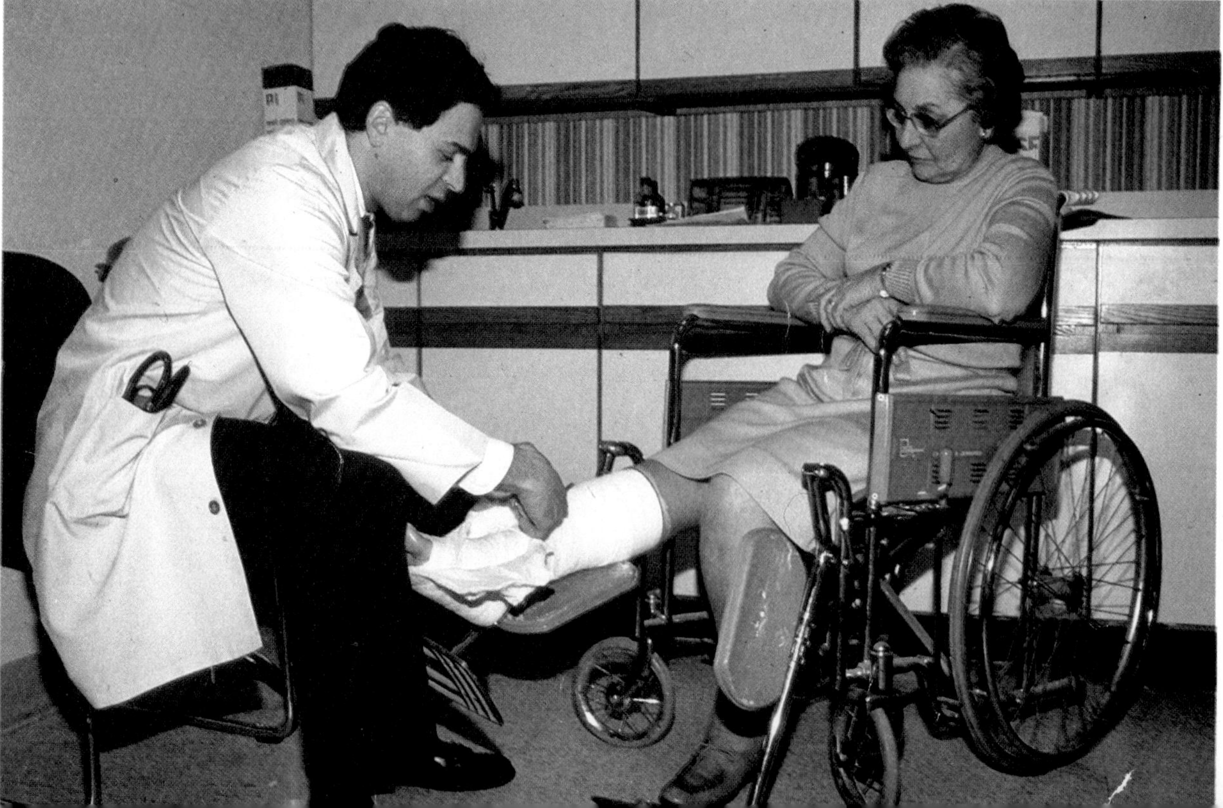

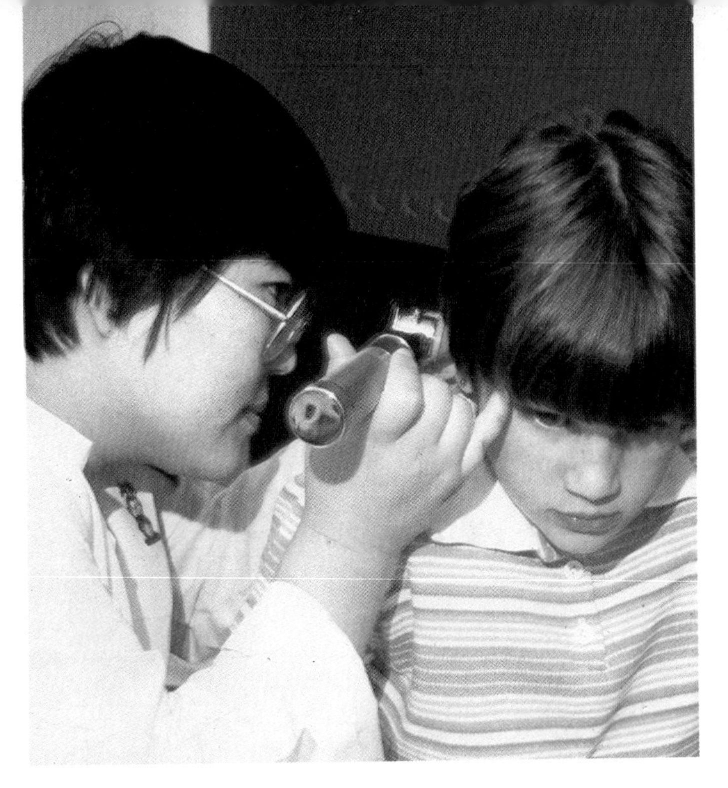

Doctors take care of sick people. They also know how to help healthy people stay healthy.

There are many different kinds of doctors.

There are eye doctors, bone doctors, and ear, nose, and throat doctors.

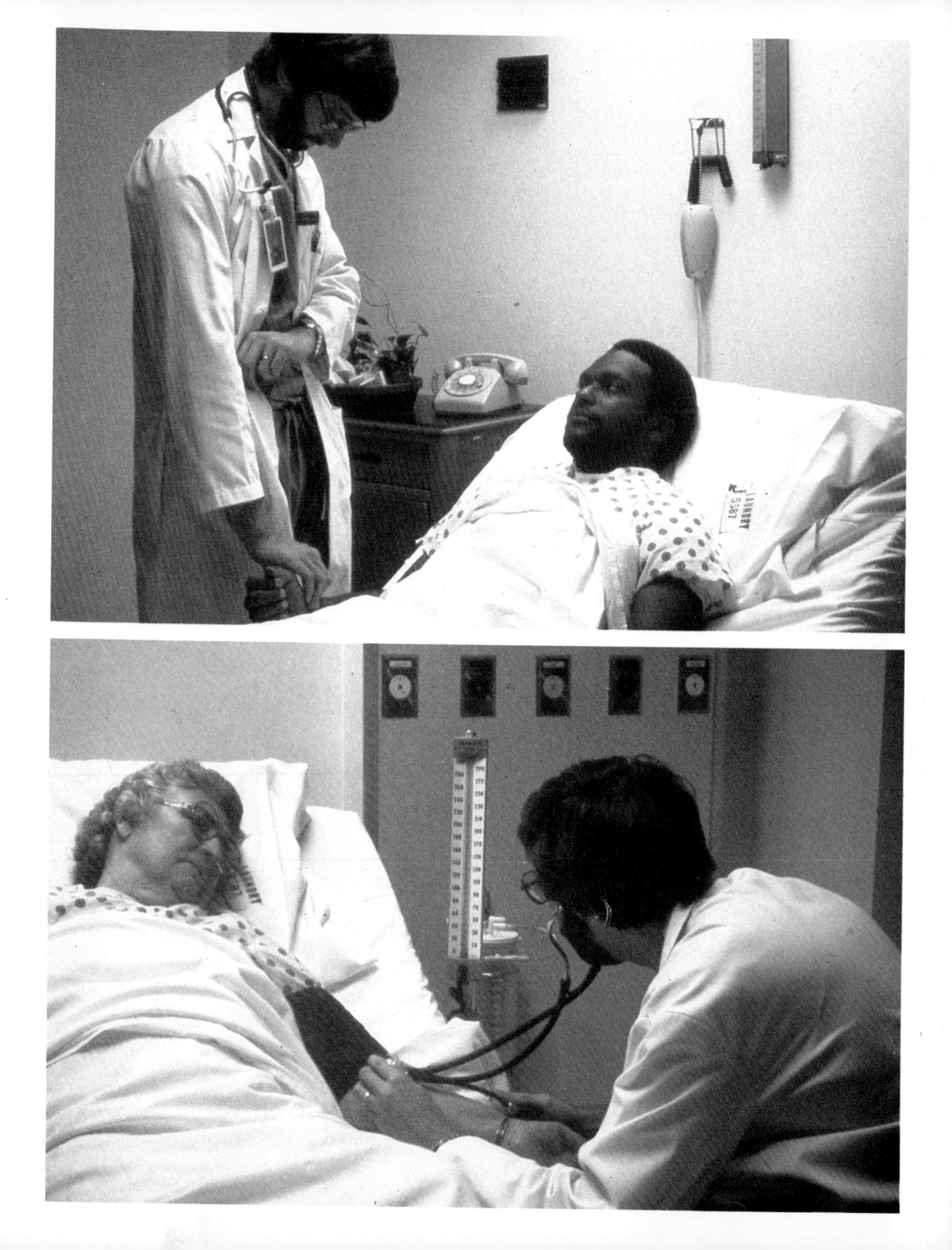
LAUNDRY
5387

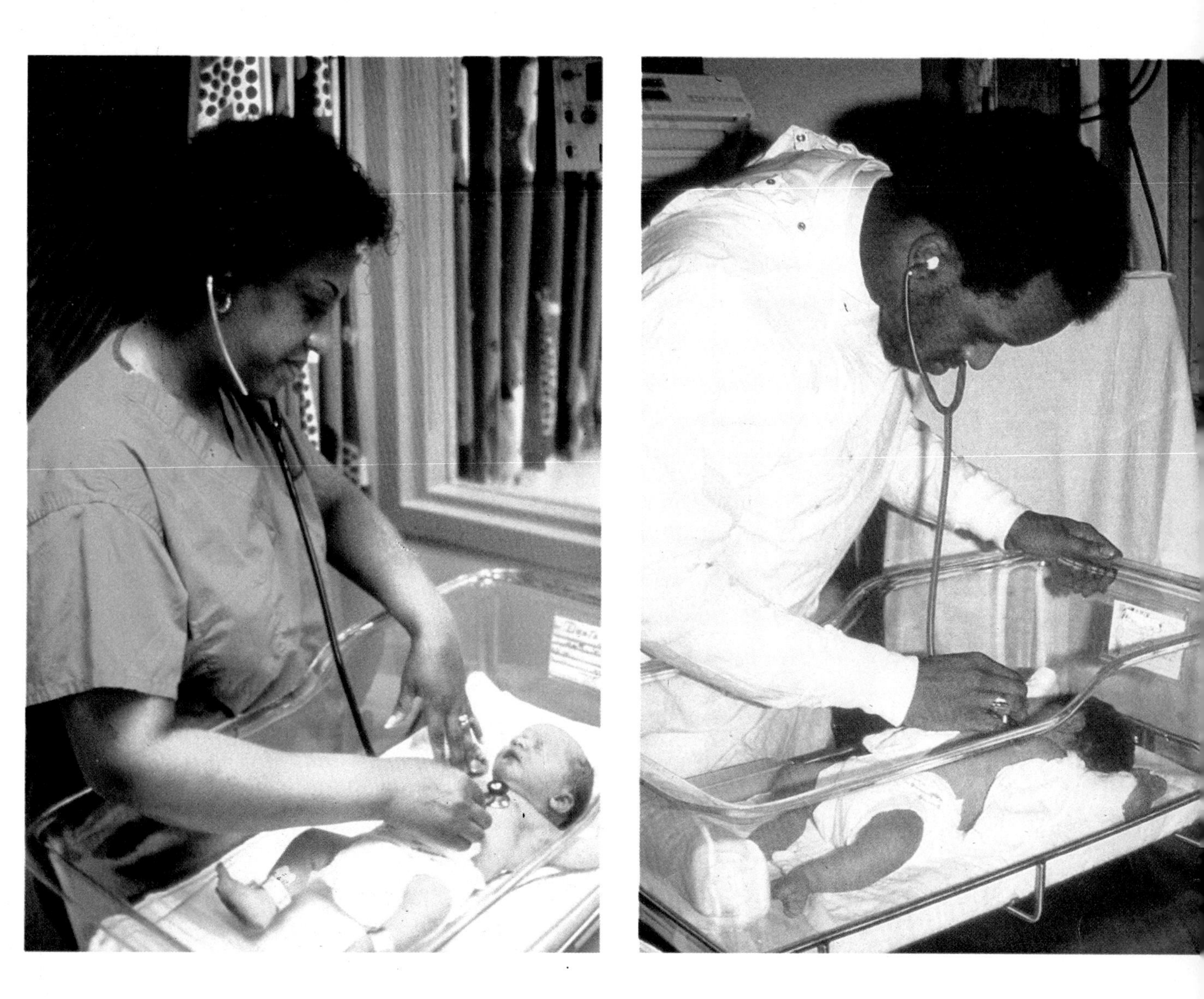

Some doctors take care of children only.

Still other doctors care for people of all ages.

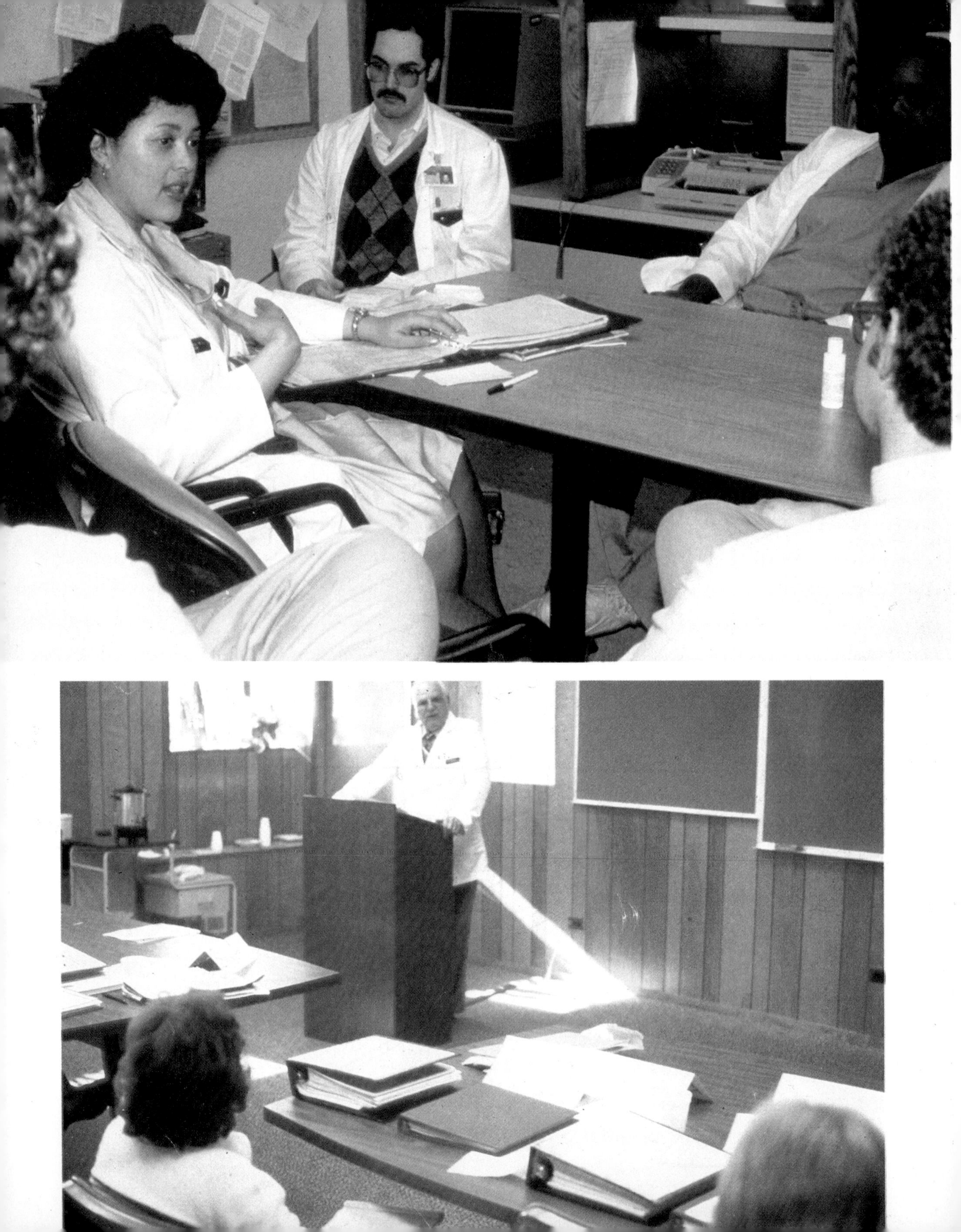

People who want to become doctors must study for many years.

First they go to college. Then they go to a special school called a medical school. In school they learn all about illnesses. They learn how the body works.

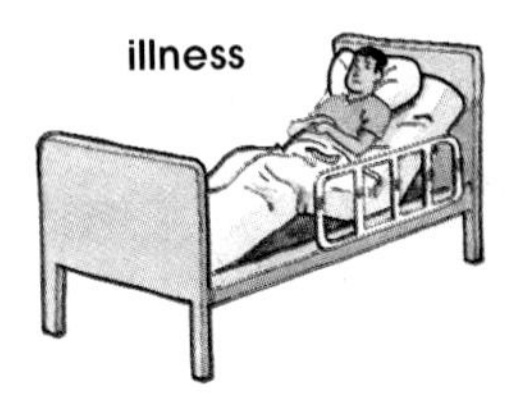

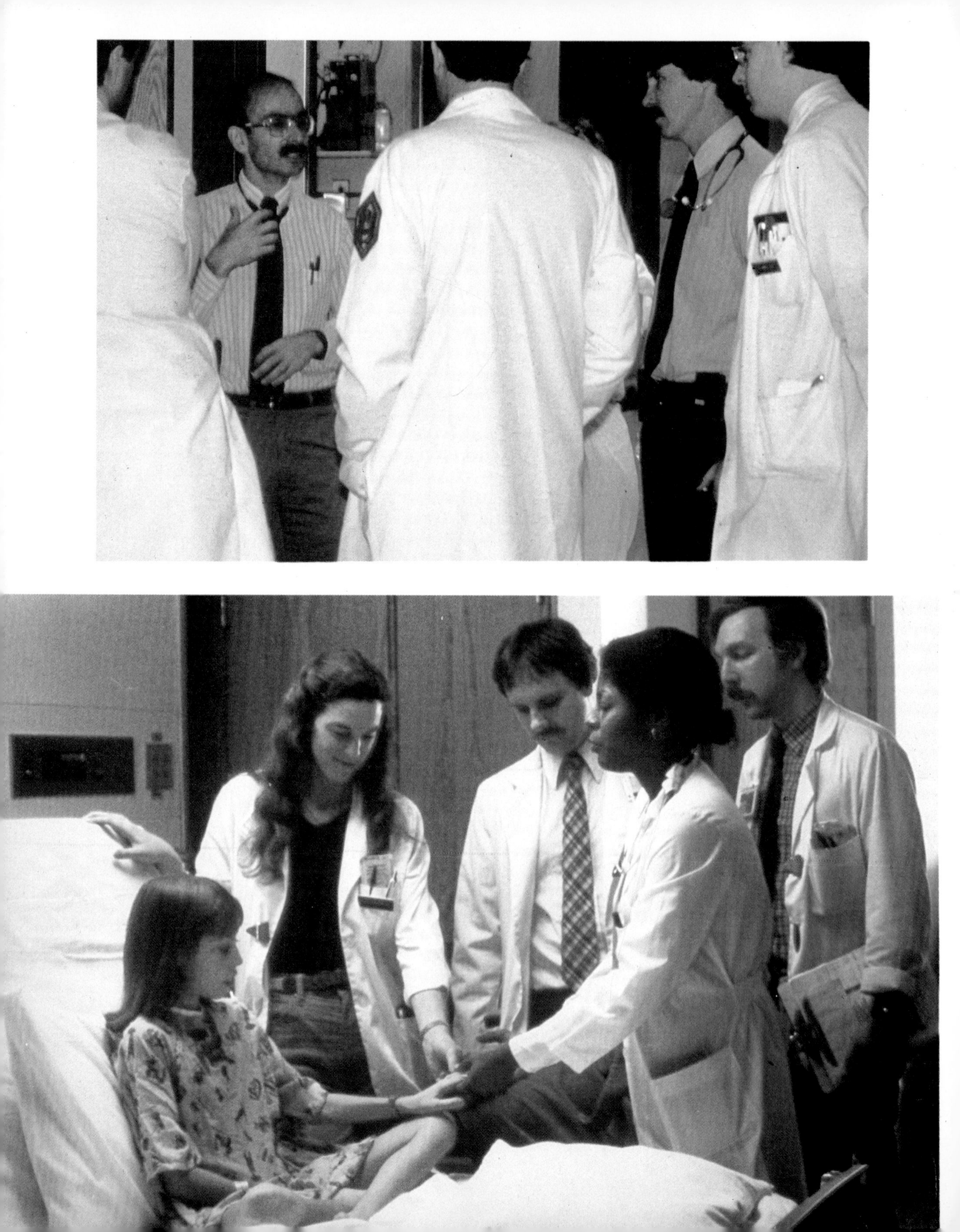

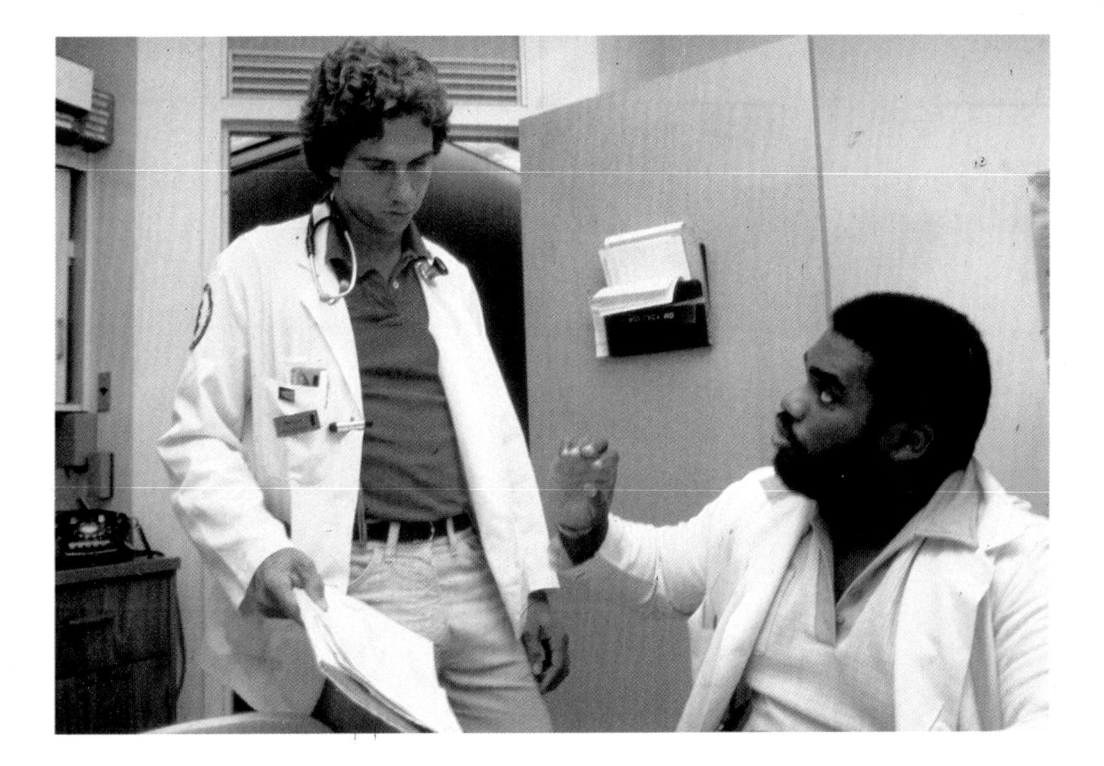

After medical school, student doctors work at hospitals. Older doctors help them take care of real patients. The young doctors learn more ways to help people get well and stay well.

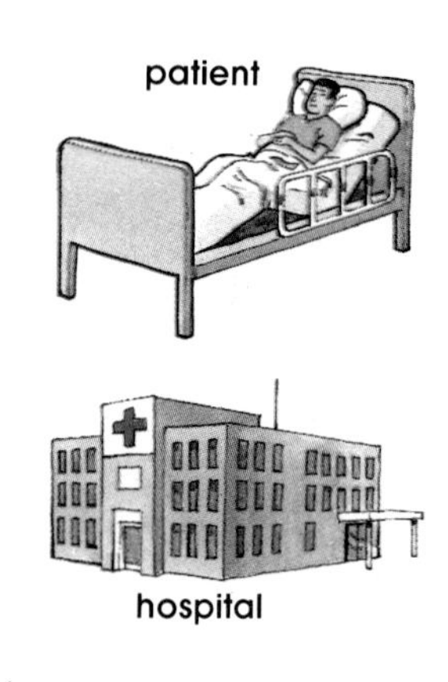

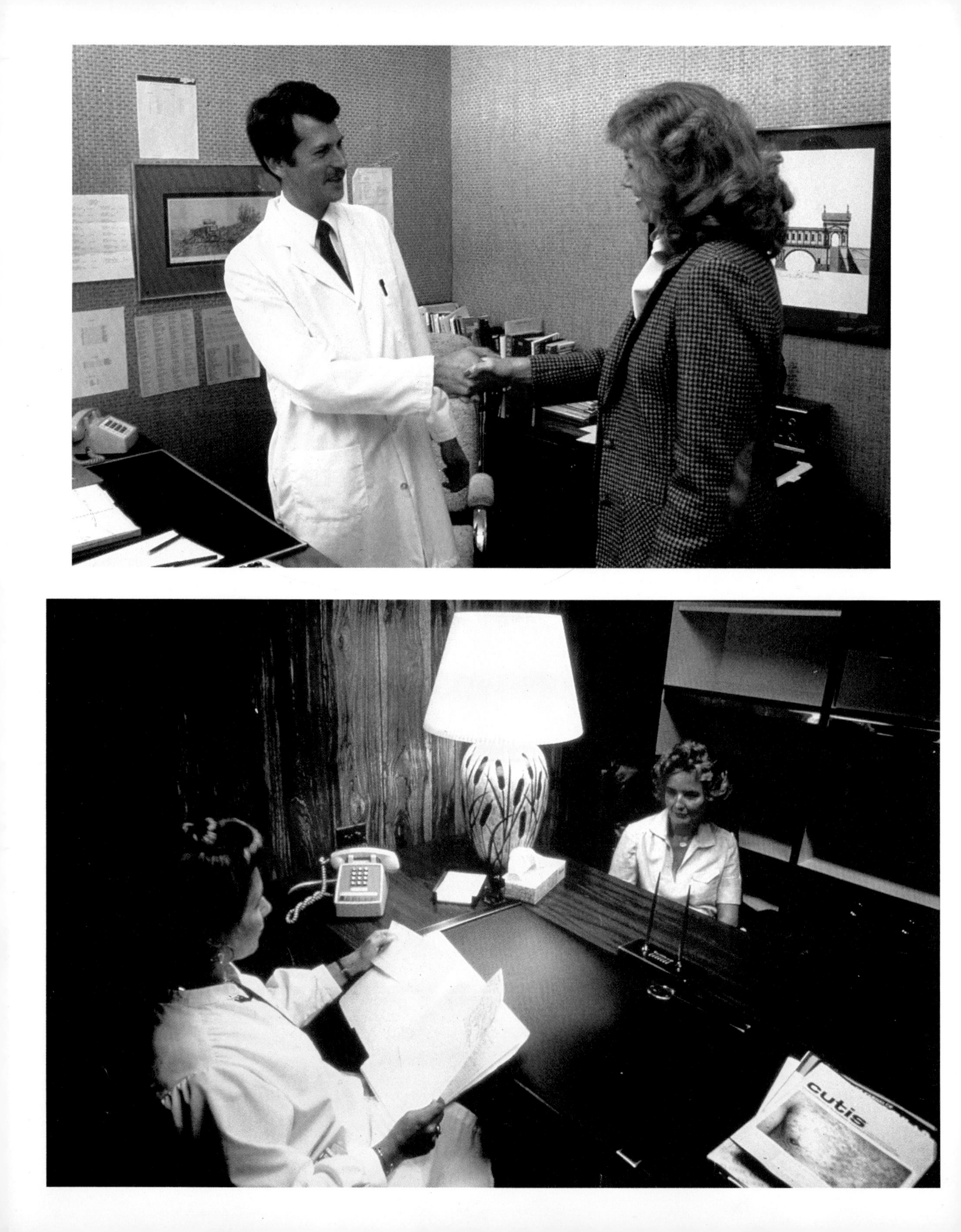
cutis

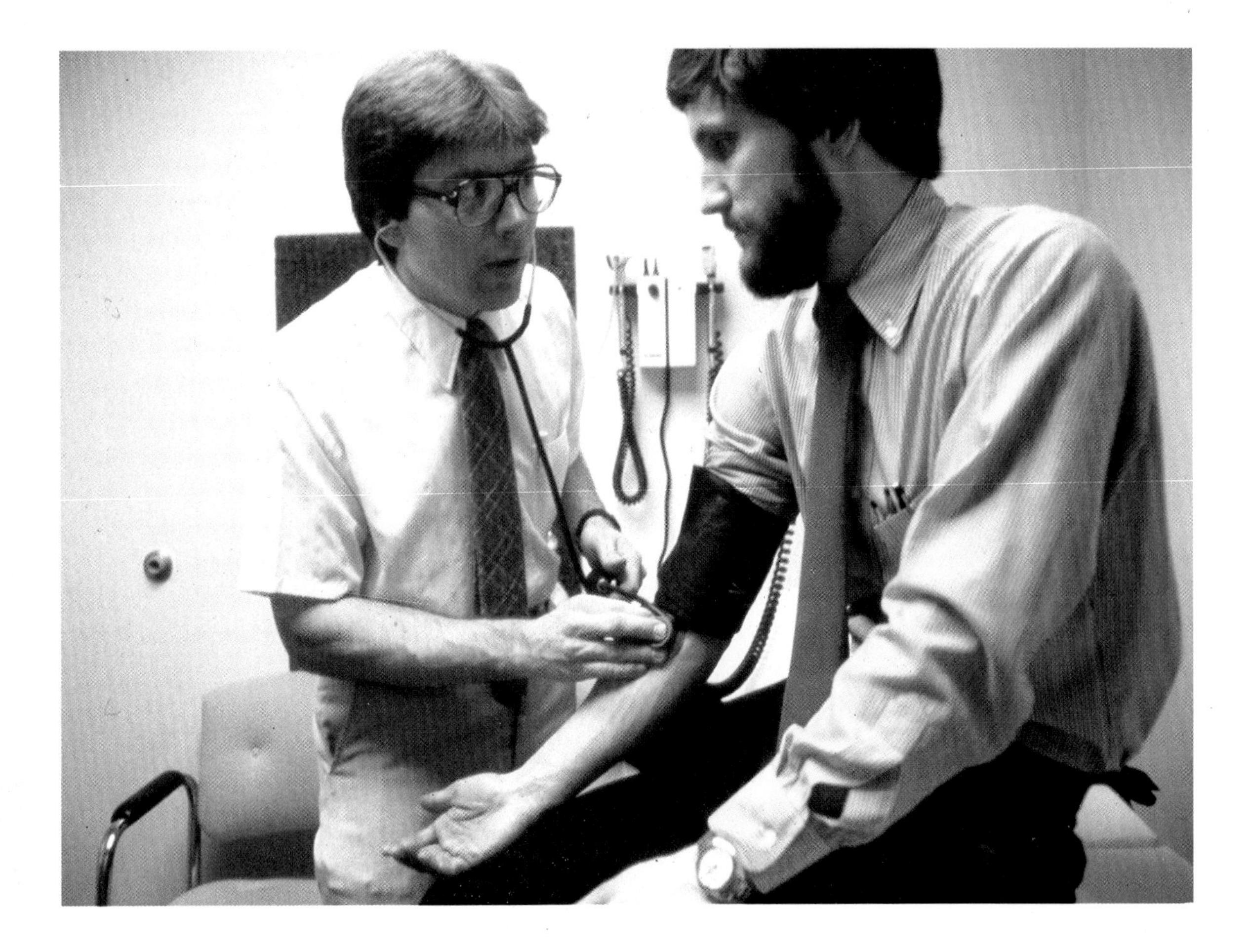

Many doctors have offices where patients come to see them. They use special tools to see and hear how a patient is doing.

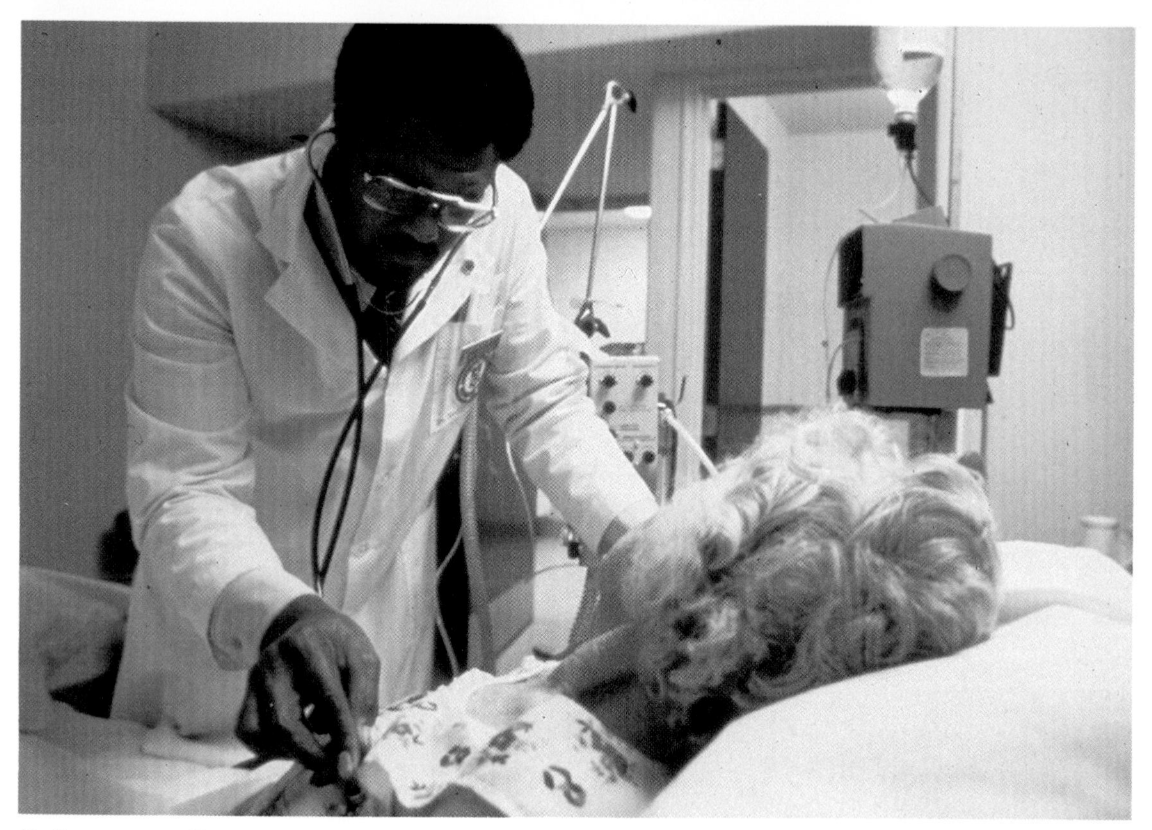

Stethoscopes (STETH • uh • skohpz)

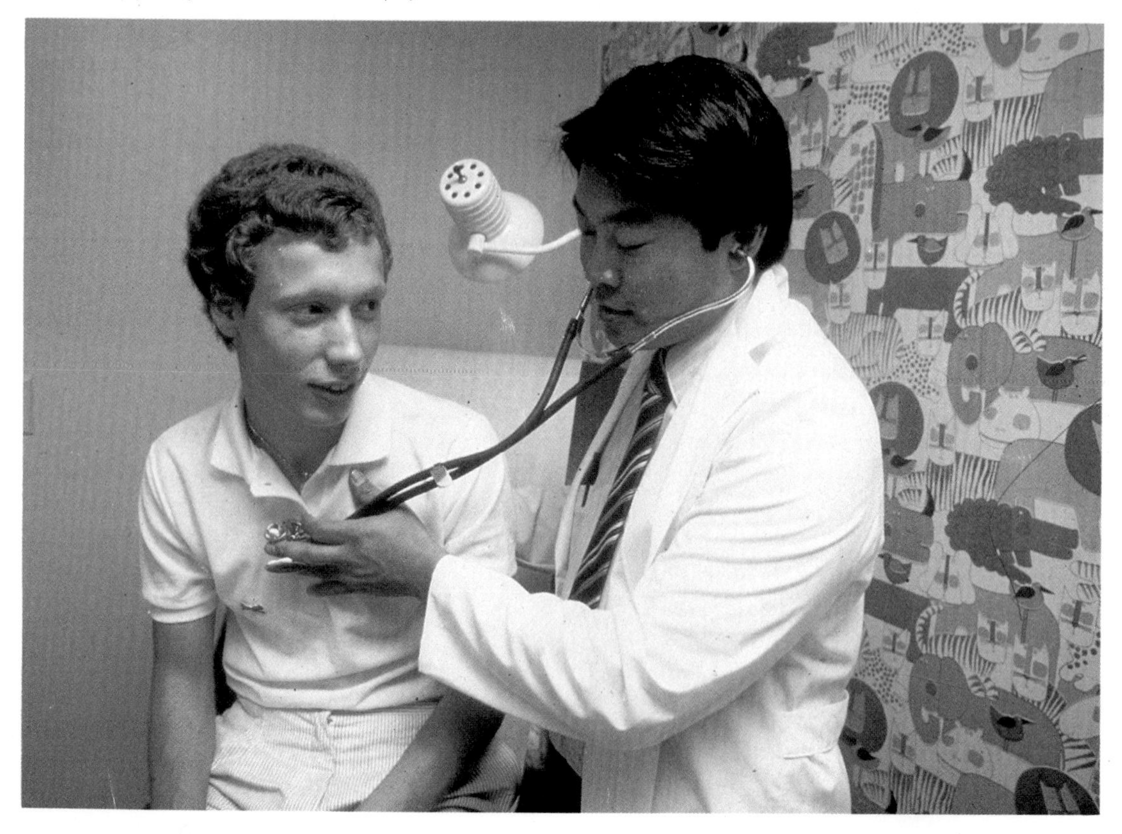

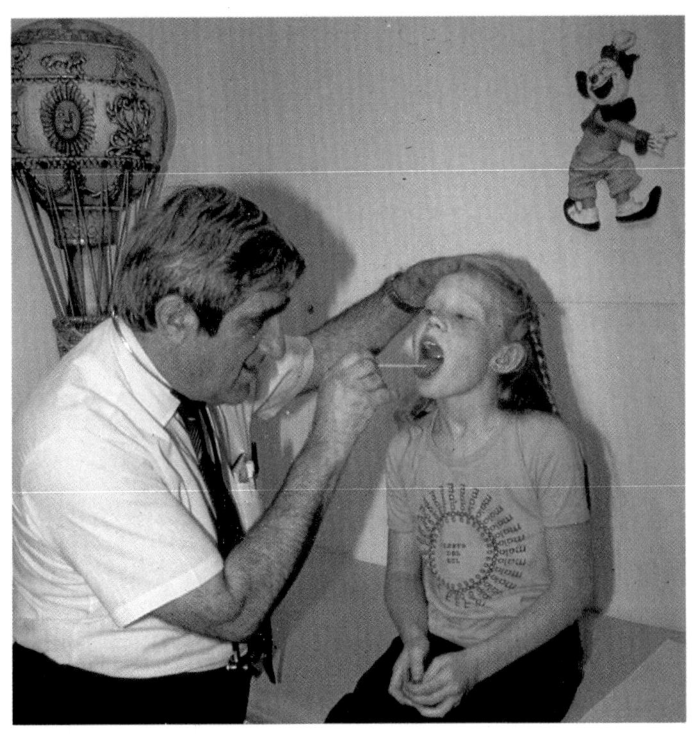

Tongue depressor

A stethoscope lets a doctor listen to your heart and lungs.

A special stick called a tongue depressor helps a doctor hold down your tongue. This lets the doctor look at your throat.

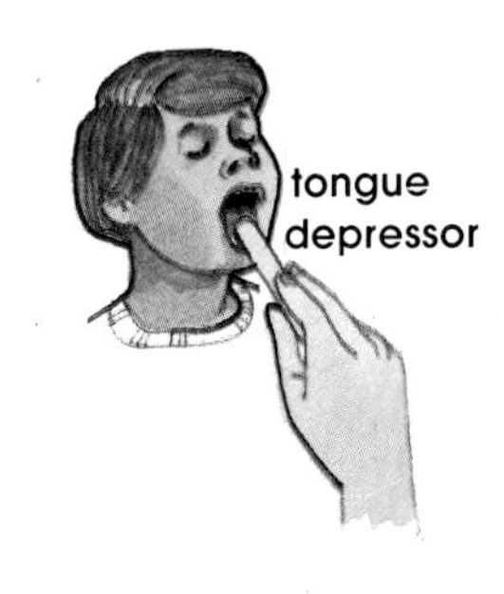

Thermometer
(ther • MOM • ih • ter)

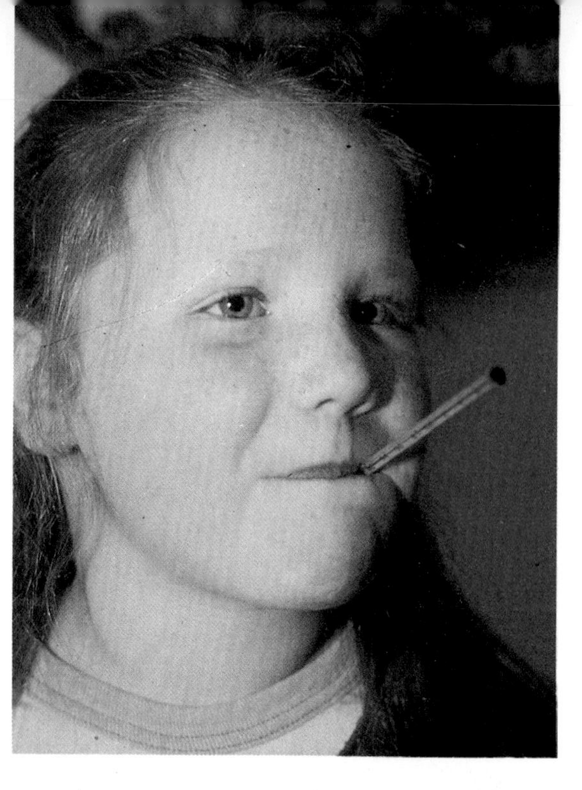

A thermometer tells a doctor if you have a fever.

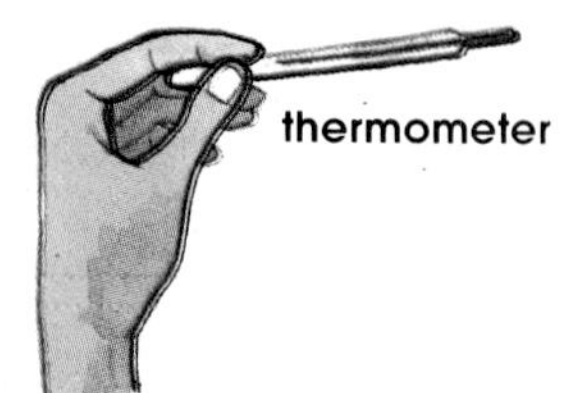

By using tools and by asking questions about how you are feeling, a doctor finds out if something is wrong with your body.

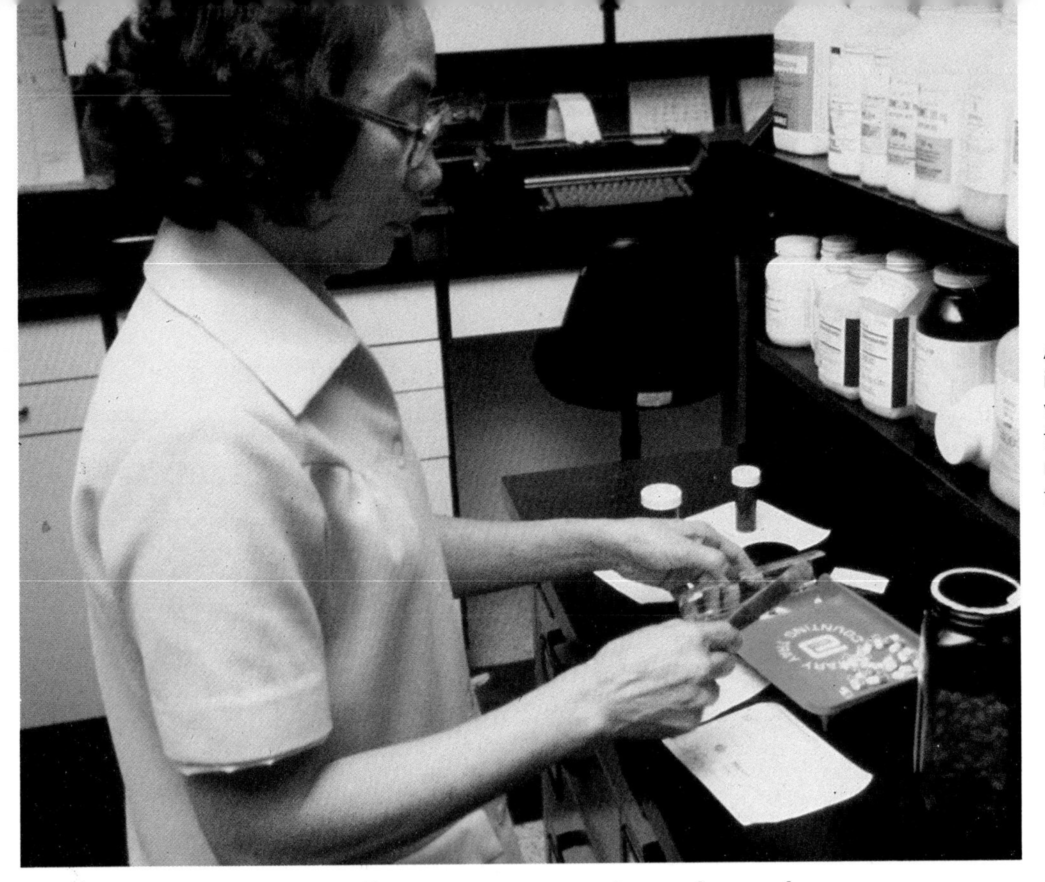

A pharmacist
is a person
who is
trained to
make the medicine
the doctor orders.

Once a doctor knows what is wrong, he or she can decide what needs to be done.

A doctor might write an order for a special medicine. This order is called a prescription.

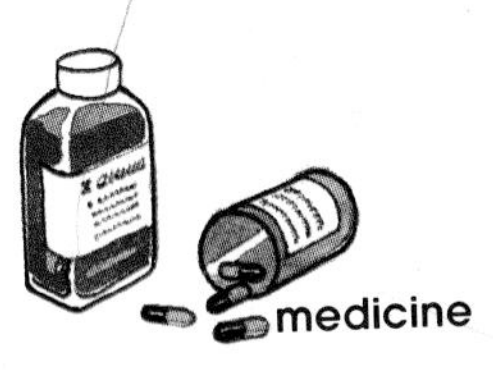

A doctor tells a young boy what will happen during his operation.

Sometimes a sick person needs an operation. This boy is going to have his tonsils out. The boy is a little scared. His doctor talks to him and makes him feel better. The boy and his parents get ready for the big day. They pack a small suitcase and go to the hospital the night before the operation.

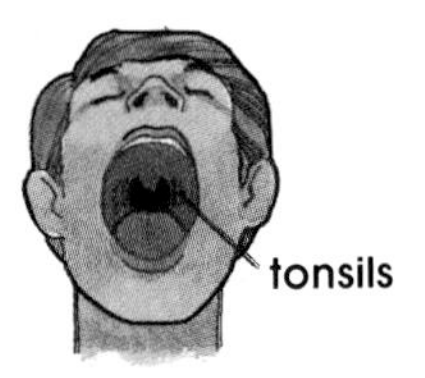

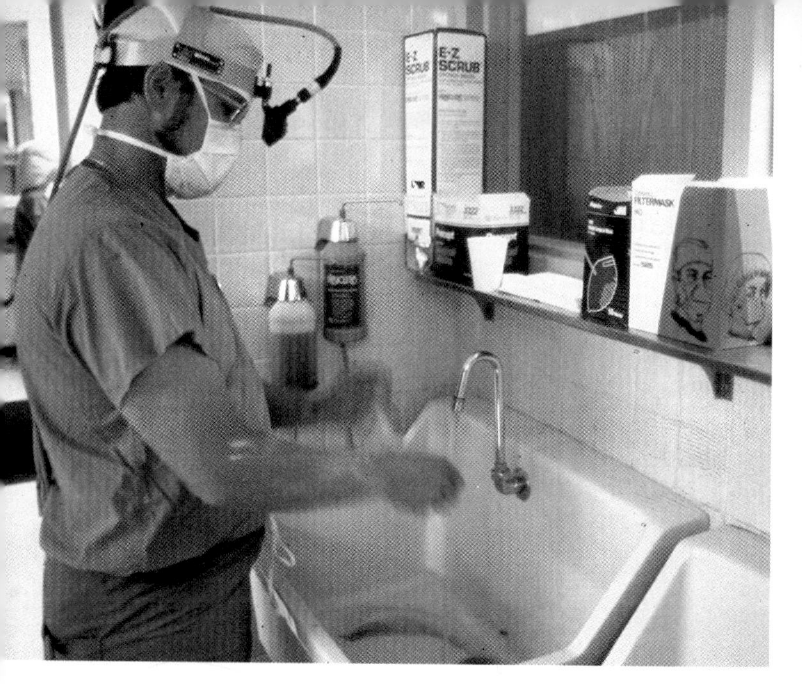

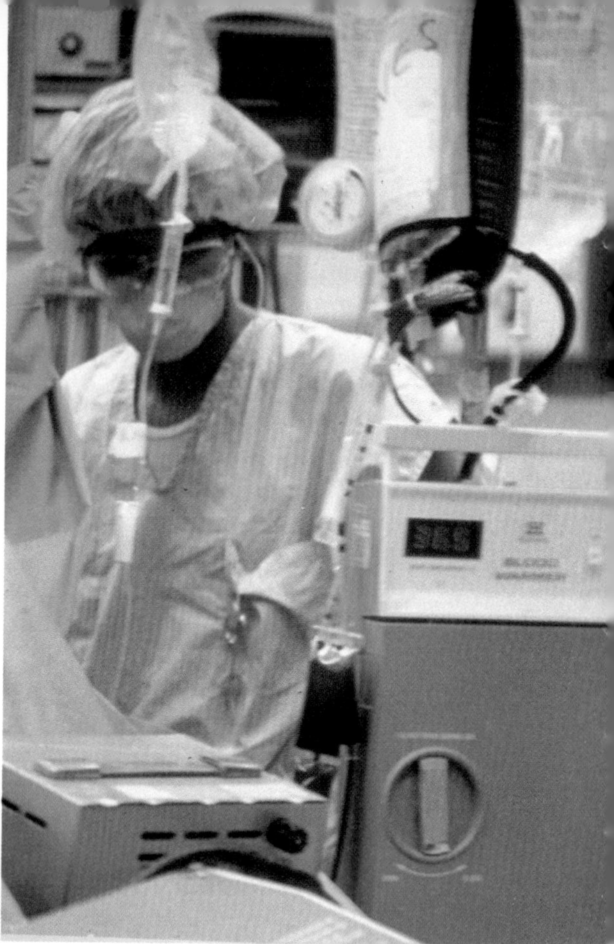

Many people help the doctor in the operating room. They must scrub their hands and arms. They wear special clothes and masks to keep the operating room free from germs.

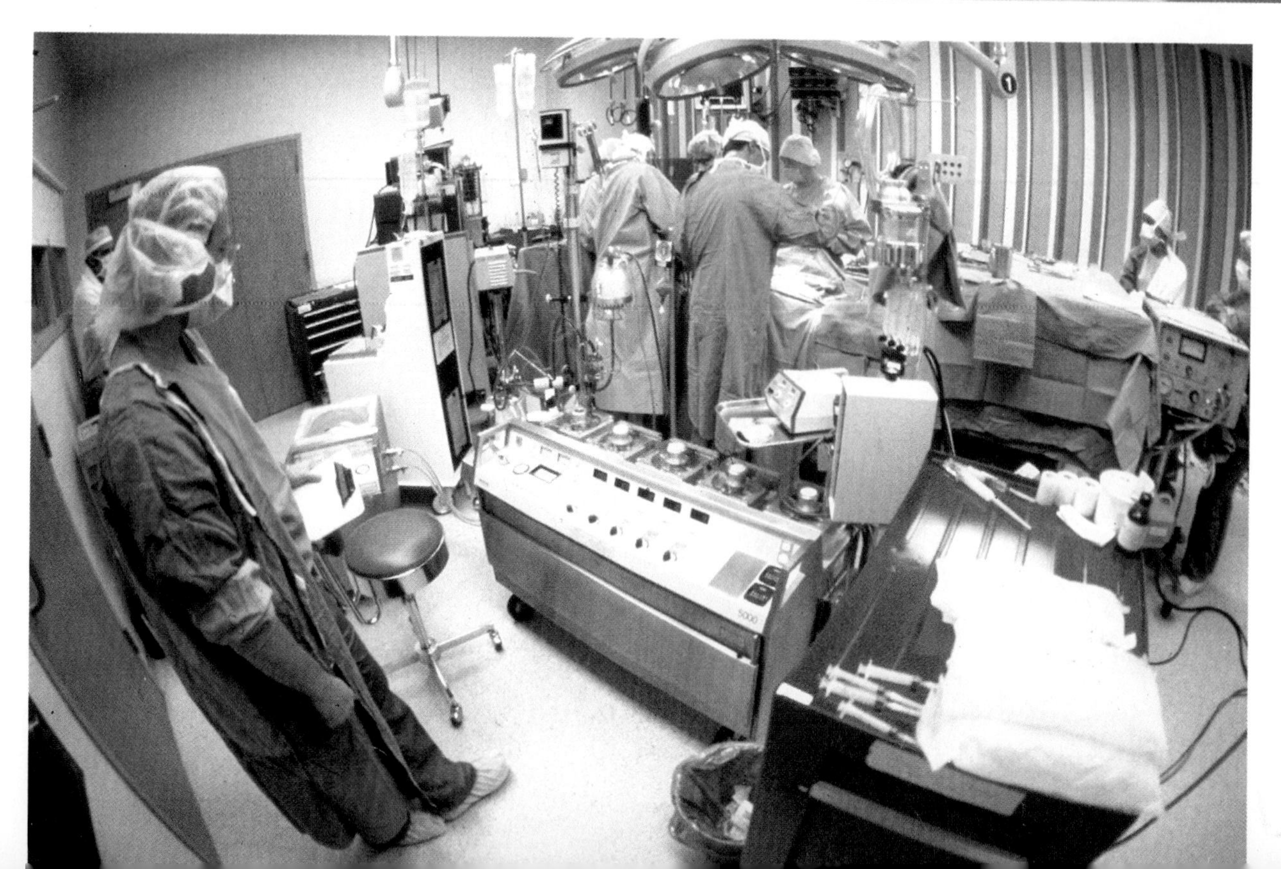

The next morning, the boy is taken to the operating room.

A special doctor called an anesthesiologist gives him something to make him sleep. While the boy is asleep his doctor will take out his tonsils.

operating room

anesthesiologist
(an•es•thee•zee•AHL•uh•jist)

When the operation is over, the doctor comes to see the boy in his room. The boy will stay in the hospital for a few days before going home.

Doctors take care of sick people. But they take care of healthy people, too.

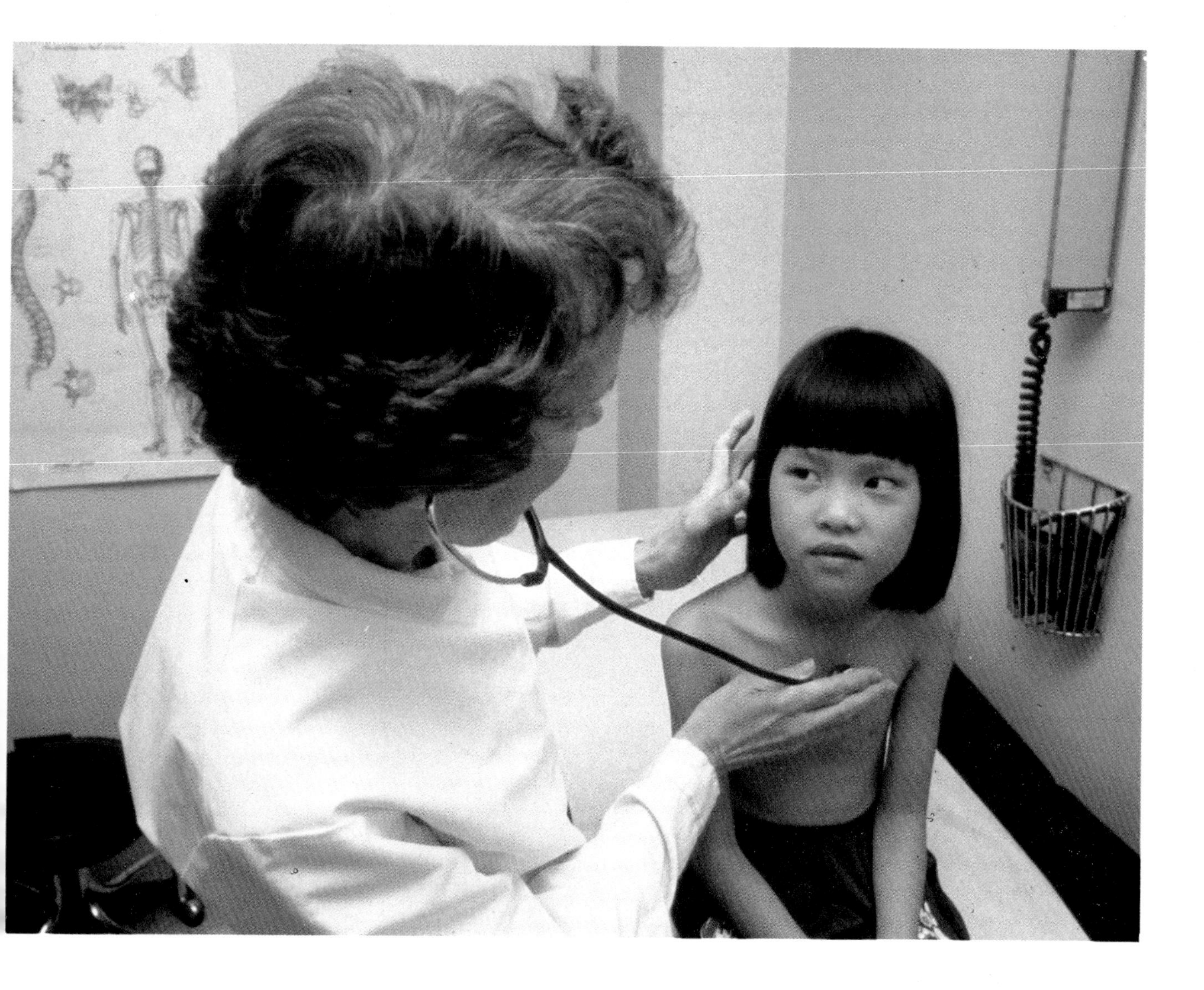

This girl is getting a checkup. Her doctor checks to make sure she is well.

checkup

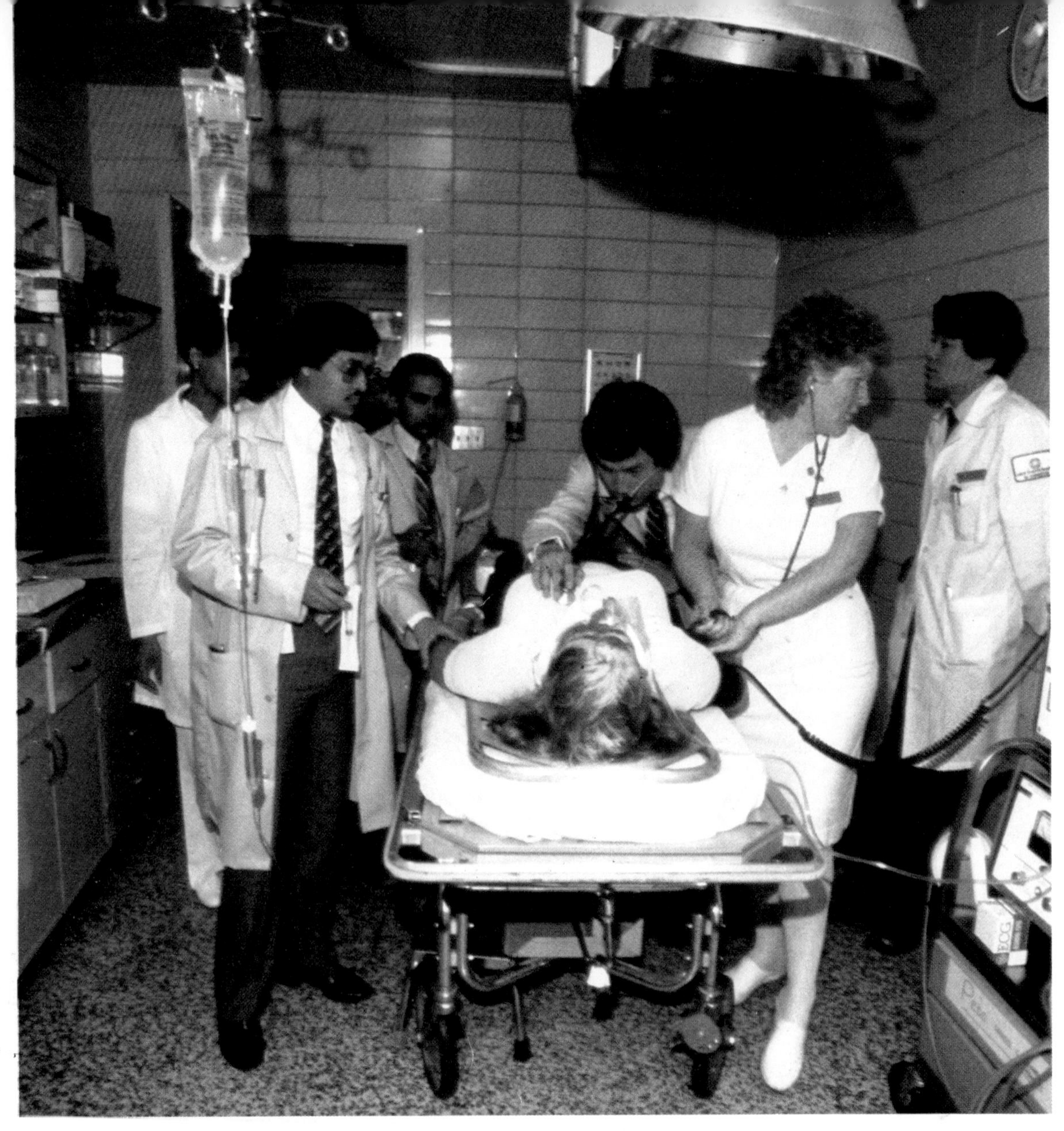

Emergency room doctors help an accident victim.

Sometimes doctors help people outside the hospital or office.

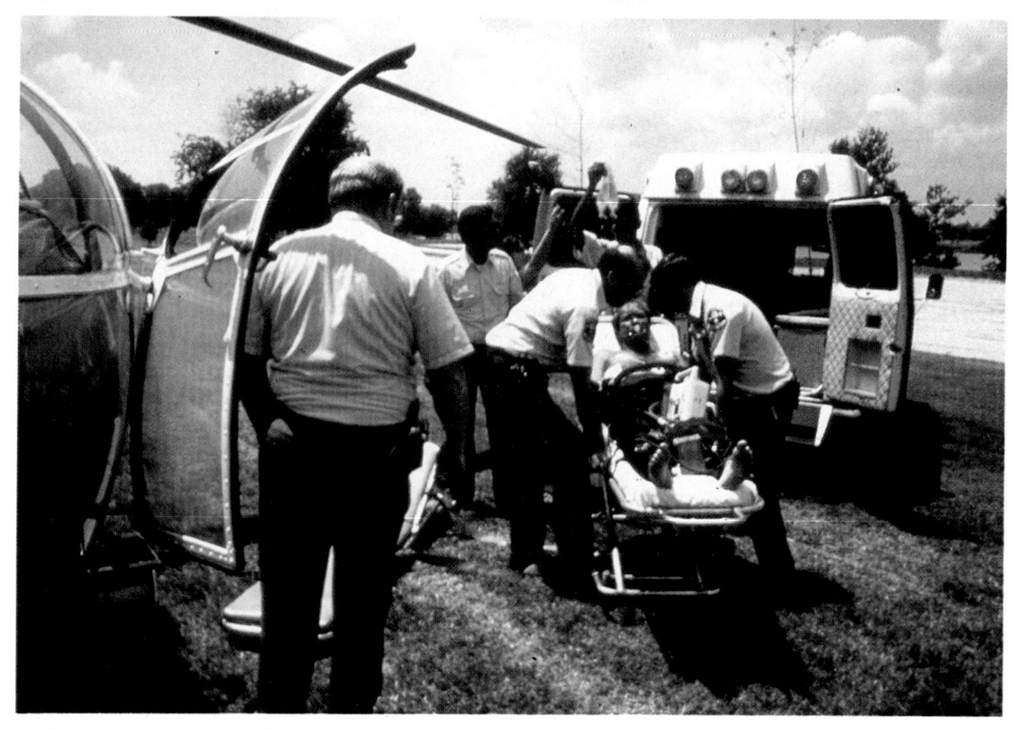

Helicopters are used to rush people to the hospital.

Accidents happen without any warning. Sometimes doctors and people who have had special training rush to help the people who are hurt. Their work can save lives.

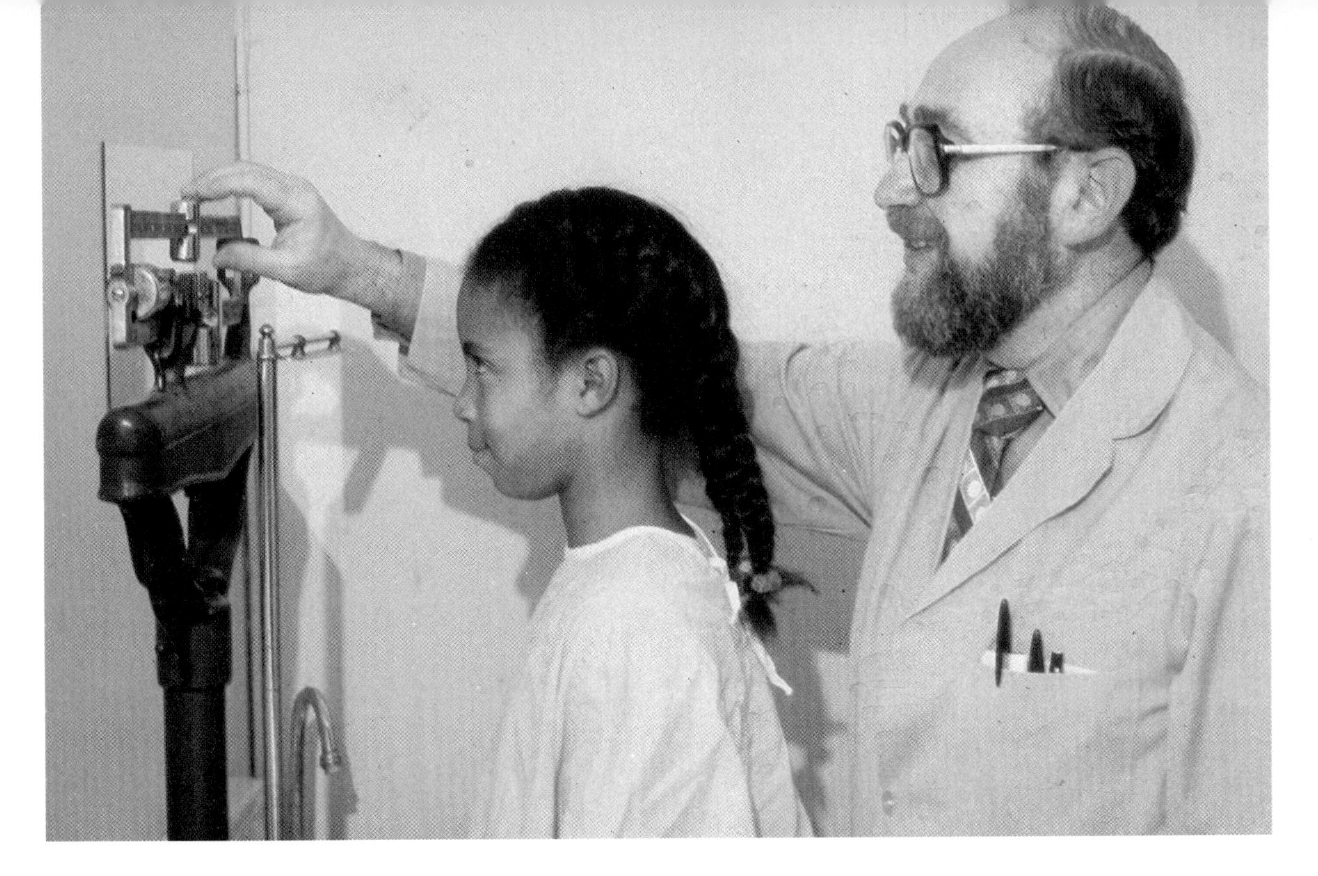

To stay healthy, people should have regular physical examinations. A doctor (above) checks his patient's weight during her checkup. X-rays (below) are used to look inside the body.

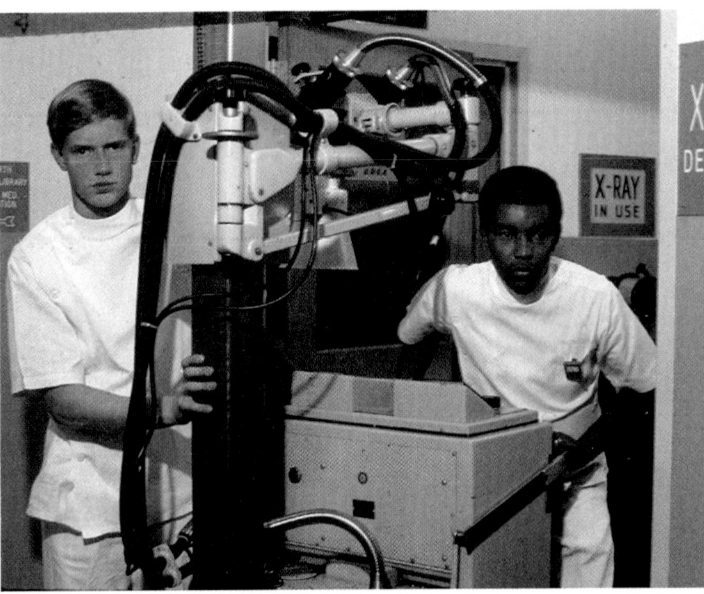

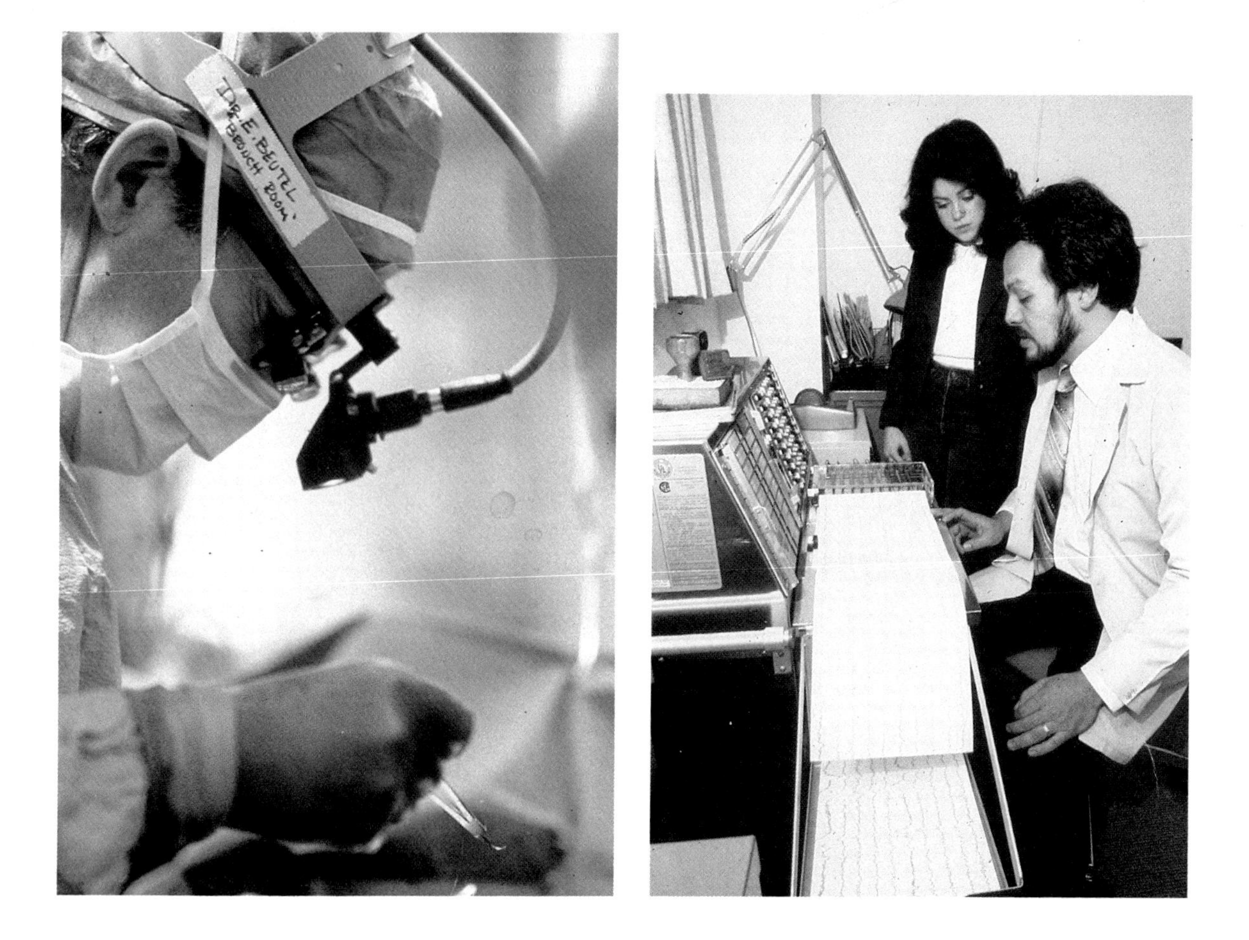

Being a doctor is hard work. But people who want to be doctors think it is worth it. They know it is important to help others.

Would you like to be a doctor?

WORDS YOU SHOULD KNOW

anesthesiologist
(an • es • thee • zee • AHL • uh • jist) —a special doctor who gives a patient something to make him or her sleep during an operation

checkup (CHEK • up)—an examination, by a doctor, that checks to see if the person really is well

college (KAHL • ij)—a school of higher learning attended by students who have graduated from high school

fever (FEE • ver)—a body temperature that is higher than normal

headache (HED • aik)—a pain or ache in the head

healthy (HELTH • ee)—having good health

hospital (HAHSS • pit • uhl)—a building where hurt or sick people are cared for by doctors and nurses

illness (IL • ness)—not healthy; sick

medical school (MED • ih • kuhl SKOOL)—a special school, attended by students who have graduated from college, if they want to become doctors

medicine (MED • ih • sin)—a substance, such as pills, capsules, and liquids, given to sick people to make them well again

operating room (OP • er • rayt • ing ROOM)—a room in a hospital where operations are performed

operation (op • er • RAY • shun)—a medical act done by a doctor who uses tools and instruments to fix the part of the body of a patient that needs help

patient (PAY • shunt)—a person who goes to see a doctor because of illness or for a checkup

prescription (pri • SKRIP • shun)—a doctor's written order for a special medicine

sick (SIK)—not healthy; ill

stethoscope (STETH • uh • skohp)—a tool used by a doctor to listen to the sounds of your heart, lungs, and other parts of the body

thermometer (ther • MOM • ih • ter)—a small tool used by a doctor to see if you have a fever

tongue depressor (TUNG • di • PRESS • er)—a small stick used by a doctor to hold down (or depress) the tongue so your throat can be seen and examined

tonsils (TAHN • sulls)—body tissues at the back of the throat. Tonsils often become infected and are taken out by a doctor in an operation

INDEX

PHOTO CREDITS

© Jacqueline Durand—Cover, 4 (bottom), 5, 6 (top), 7, 26, 28 (top), 29 (right)

Frost Publishing Group, Ltd.—28 (bottom right)
© Shands Hospital—4 (top)
© Humana, Inc.—9 (left), 27

Hillstrom Stock Photo:
© Mac Tavish—14 (top)

Nawrocki Stock Photo:
© Michael Brohm: 22 (top left and bottom), 28 (bottom left)
© Larry Brooks—10 (bottom), 13, 19, 20, 25
© Harry J. Przekop Jr.—29 (left)
© Jim Wright—15

Tom Stack and Associates:
© Don & Pat Valenti—6 (bottom)
© Ken Kaminsky—14 (bottom)

Courtesty University of Illinois Hospital—8 (2 photos), 9 right, 10 (top), 12 (2 photos), 22 (top right)

Image Finders:
© Bob Skelly—17 (2 photos)

Cover: Ophthalmologist examines a patient's eyes.

About the Author

Rebecca Hankin is a writer and editor who lives in Chicago.